Self-Regulation and the Underachieving Gifted Learner

Alicia M. Welch, Jennifer L. Roth, Hillary H. Steiner, and Martha M. Carr

Cheryll M. Adams, Series Editor

National Association for Gifted Children
1331 H Street, NW, Suite 1001
Washington, DC 20005
202-785-4268
http://www.nagc.org

TABLE OF CONTENTS

INTRODUCTION

What role does self-regulation play in achievement for gifted students? How is motivation embedded within self-regulation? According to Zimmerman,[1] self-regulated learning involves the interaction among motivational, cognitive, and social factors as they influence achievement. As such, motivation cannot be understood independent of context and student knowledge and skill. This *NAGC Select* will discuss a model of self-regulation that explains how metacognitive skills and motivation interact to affect achievement and how problems with self-regulation may contribute to underachievement in gifted students. Potential causes of underachievement that are related to self-regulation are discussed with recommended interventions. The cases of Harper and Steven, examples of two gifted high school students who have experienced underachievement, are discussed in light of the research on self-regulation. At the end we revisit their cases to discuss how their outcomes may be improved through self-regulated learning interventions. While high school students are used in the case studies and as the focus for the interventions, these interventions could be easily adapted for use with younger students.

Case 1: Harper

Harper, who was identified as gifted in third grade, has performed well on every standardized test she has ever taken. She is extremely creative, witty, and demonstrates high ability in activities both inside and outside of school. Her success in school has always occurred with little effort. Harper, now a senior in high school, is currently ranked fifth in her graduating class, and she is taking what would be a very challenging course load for the average student. She has always enjoyed mathematics and is taking calculus with Mr. Perry who also taught her pre-calculus the previous school year. While Harper has always been successful in

1

mathematics in the past, she has recently begun to struggle. Mr. Perry has noticed a new lack of confidence in Harper as well as symptoms of test anxiety. She seems not to understand the concepts, but she has high expectations for herself and believes she should make an A on every test and should perform better than her peers. Harper is very competitive and feels defeated when her expectations aren't met. She feels pressure from Mr. Perry, her parents, and herself, which exacerbate her feelings of frustration and lack of confidence. In pre-calculus, she often did not complete her homework, but this did not affect her grade. Now, however, her failure to complete assignments seems to be affecting her performance, and she has begun to associate her failure with lack of ability. Mr. Perry is very concerned because Harper seems to be giving up and he would like to find some strategies to help Harper become more successful.

Case 2: Steven

Steven, who was identified as gifted in fifth grade, began to show signs of struggle in eighth grade. He had always made As and Bs in the past, but he fell to mostly Bs and Cs in eighth grade. Currently he is failing his ninth grade literature class, claiming he does not enjoy reading or writing. Mrs. Torres, Steven's literature teacher, is frustrated with Steven because he is disorganized, does not complete assignments, often loses his assigned reading books, does not pay attention in class, does not take notes, and disrupts class through constant conversations with his peers. Mrs. Torres is most annoyed by the fact that Steven seems completely unconcerned. Steven is very charming and has many friends; his social life seems to be much more important than his schoolwork. When Steven received his recent progress report, he seemed surprised. He told Mrs. Torres that he really thought he was doing much better and responded with a seemingly infinite list of excuses as to why he is doing so poorly.

Research on self-regulated learning and gifted underachievers has been helpful in exploring reasons why students like Harper and Steven experience underachievement and with developing effective interventions aimed at helping these students. In short, self-regulated learners are metacognitively, motivationally, and behaviorally active participants in their own learning. They plan, organize, set goals, self-monitor, self-evaluate, attribute success to effort rather than ability, optimize their learning environments, and report high levels of self-efficacy, feelings of control, and intrinsic task interest.[2] They are also aware of the relationship between their regulatory processes and achievement, and they are aware of how they use strategies to achieve their goals. Another feature of self-regulation is the feedback loop, in which students self-monitor and make changes in their self-perceptions and behavior.[3] Such a feedback loop allows for students to choose and monitor behaviors in order to help them meet their goals. Such behaviors may be based upon their beliefs about themselves as learners, which in turn affect future behaviors.

Teachers usually have high expectations for their gifted students, but some gifted students lack the motivation to learn and do little to regulate their learning. Underachievement in gifted students can be short lived, occurring in a particular subject area, or it can be chronic, occurring time after time within one area or across multiple areas of study.[4] While high-achieving gifted students usually use more self-regulated learning strategies than other students, the gifted underachiever may not. Fortunately, self-regulatory processes are teachable, and students who use them can improve their academic achievement.[5]

3

PORTRAIT OF THE UNDERACHIEVING GIFTED STUDENT

Underachievement in a gifted child is often surprising and disheartening for parents and teachers who see a mismatch between the child's performance and potential. Underachievement can present itself in a variety of ways related to self-regulation, including a general lack of motivation, a struggle with basic academic tasks, or poor academic self-discipline. It also may become problematic at any time in a gifted child's life, often surfacing during times of increased academic challenge, such as the transition from high school to college. This section provides an overview of underachievement in gifted students and discusses characteristics often found in gifted underachievers.

Underachievement is rather ill defined in the literature. Most define it as a discrepancy between achievement and potential ability, but the difficulty in operationalizing these terms means definitions differ slightly from study to study.[6] For example, potential ability can be demonstrated by a child's extracurricular activities or interests, evidence of precocious thinking, witty sense of humor, or exceptional standardized test scores. These are typical characteristics of gifted children that lead teachers and parents to expect good grades and high academic motivation. When these expectations are not met, and achievement does not match potential, the child might be considered to be an underachiever. Similarly, underachievers might show great creativity and ability in activities outside of school, yet fail to perform as expected on similar tasks within a school setting. This kind of paradoxical behavior is distressing to parents and teachers who see the potential for greatness.

While beyond the scope of this *NAGC Select*, an important consideration is the possibility of twice-exceptionality. Twice-exceptional (2e) students are gifted or high-ability students who also have a disability such as a learning disability, attention deficit hyperactivity disorder, a behavioral disorder, or autism spectrum disorder.[7] In many cases, a disability may go undiagnosed as symptoms are masked by a student's high ability or compensating behavior. Similarly, a 2e student's giftedness may be masked by a disability and go unidentified. In either case, gifted students may exhibit high ability in one area but struggle in another making it appear as though they are underachieving when, in fact, their disability is undermining their performance.

Underachievement among gifted students is more widespread than commonly thought. Some estimates suggest that up to a quarter of high school dropouts are gifted underachievers, but the actual number might be much higher due to the difficulty in establishing a student's potential via a performance-based assessment.[8] For example, when tests of ability are used to measure a student's potential, underachievers who underperform on these types of standardized tests may not be identified as gifted even though they show potential in other ways.[9] Furthermore, students who underachieve often fall further behind in school and after years of repetitive underachievement may not be seen by their teachers as having high potential at all[10] and are often overlooked for gifted andtalented programs.

Traits

Gifted underachievers are not a homogenous group. Characteristics of underachievers vary, but there are several common traits that parents and teachers may notice that should prompt further evaluation. Beyond the potential/performance discrepancy, there are less obvious motivational characteristics that are seen in gifted underachievers of all ages. Many of these traits are related to self-regulation, and go unnoticed until the student reaches an area of challenge where self-regulatory abilities are necessary for success.

Reis and McCoach[11] provided a comprehensive review of the literature on underachieving gifted students and note several personal and affective traits common to underachievers. For example, gifted underachievers often have lower self-efficacy than higher achievers. They do not see themselves as gifted students and may feel incapable of performing like them, especially on tasks that are "traditionally" academic, such as test taking and practice work. Many have test anxiety or poor test-taking skills, which can further reinforce the belief that they do not measure up. Robert Sternberg, a psychologist known best in the gifted community for his triarchic theory of intelligence, is an excellent example of this type of underachieving gifted student. A bright child but a poor test-taker, he was placed into an academic track for low achievers, where he stayed for many years. Teacher after teacher gave him the message that he was not successful. In college for example, his weak performance in introductory psychology prompted his advisor to suggest another major. His distaste and low self-efficacy for traditional academic tasks caused him to think about learning and intelligence in a new way, eventually leading him to develop theories of intelligence that go beyond measuring achievement and intellectual ability and prompting him to enter the very field he was discouraged to pursue.

Many underachievers are also weak in their ability to set appropriate academic goals.[12] Because learning comes easily, gifted students often do not develop study skills when they are young. For these students, summarizing, underlining, and self-testing are unnecessary for learning. It is likely, that they have not yet needed to think about how to best study. It might not be until high school or college when they are sufficiently academically challenged that they need to acquire these regulatory skills. If parents or teachers are not aware of the need to develop these skills, gifted children may increasingly underachieve as they continue to study using techniques that are not effective.

Ironically, gifted students are often told that they are "naturally smart." This, in combination with the ease of learning in elementary school, may cause gifted students to believe that ability is innate and inflexible. Many gifted underachievers have maladaptive beliefs about learning that influence their behavior. Attributing failures to ability or uncontrollable factors rather than effort leads many students to believe that academic challenges are insurmountable and thus not worth attempting.[13] This also occurs with gifted students who are more likely to self-handicap when innate ability is highlighted.[14] Any effort required for success can be seen as a sign of low ability; failure that follows high effort is especially hurtful. A common tactic for avoiding failure following high effort is to set unrealistically elevated goals, effectively setting themselves up for failure. When these goals are not met, their loftiness becomes an easy excuse for failure. "How could I have possibly achieved that high of a test score?" they reason, "I had no chance."

How Underachievement Emerges

Sylvia Rimm, a longtime advocate for underachieving gifted students, notes that underachievers often begin school as young children with great enthusiasm and imagination, yet at some point this passion wanes, often due to increased competition or dissatisfaction with the school environment.[15] They begin to find little extrinsic or intrinsic value in school and begin putting forth less effort, rebelling against teachers, and failing to turn in assignments. This failure to complete tasks is another salient characteristic of underachievement that is related to self-regulation. Rimm suggests that many bright students *learn* to underachieve as this pattern takes hold. With repeated failure, they develop defenses and inaccurate attributions, which are the explanations that students give for their successes or failures and which can help deflect the blame from themselves. The problem then worsens with parental pressure and disappointment.

As noted above, Dweck[16] has explained the underachiever's avoidance behaviors as being partially due to a fixed mindset on intelligence. That is, many underachievers believe that their abilities will not change; therefore, there is little they can do to improve. Some take this idea to the extreme, developing learned helplessness. Feeling a lack of personal control, students simply give up. Other avoidance behaviors of underachievers that teachers might notice include rebellion against school activities or creative evasion of academic tasks. "J.P.," an 8-year-old gifted underachiever described in Hettinger and Knapp,[17] struggled in learning to read and felt there was little he could do to remedy the situation. In order to regain some control over his circumstances, J.P. began escaping any settings that involved reading—even making himself sick in order to visit the school nurse. His negative view of teachers, built over years of disappointment, caused him to blame them for his reading failures. In his mind, the only thing he could do was to avoid the situation.

While underachievement can take many forms, it can be challenging to the teachers and parents who work with such students. Because many of these traits of gifted underachievers are related to self-regulation, the next section will include an in-depth discussion of Zimmerman's[18] model of self-regulated learning and how it relates to gifted underachievers. The last section focuses on interventions teachers can implement to improve the self-regulatory abilities, which are necessary for these students to achieve success.

SELF-REGULATED LEARNING

Self-regulation is a dynamic, multidimensional system that involves monitoring and controlling cognitive and behavioral strategies to reach set goals. It is not simply a group of test-taking strategies, time-management, or study skills. It is also not solely an isolated process but, rather, relies on "modeling, guidance, and feedback from peers, coaches, and teachers"[19] (p. 1). Theorists may differ with regard to the areas within self-regulation they choose for research focus, but Boekaerts and Corno[20] contend that there are shared basic assumptions about self-regulation. One shared assumption is the idea that self-regulation allows students to adapt "their thoughts, feelings, and actions as needed to affect their learning and motivation" (p. 201).

Phases of Self-Regulation

This section looks more closely at the phases of self-regulation as defined by Zimmerman[21] and related research on gifted students. Zimmerman's three cyclical phases of self-regulated learning are forethought, performance, and self-reflection, with each phase comprised of multiple components. While there is an order to the phases, students might cycle back and forth between two phases before moving on the next. Specific examples of how to apply this model to gifted students are provided in the final section.

Forethought phase. The forethought phase occurs as students prepare to perform a particular task. Forethought involves two processes: task-analysis and self-motivation.[22] Task-analysis is students' determination of what resources are available to them for this task, their beliefs about their abilities, their goals, and what needs to be done in order to

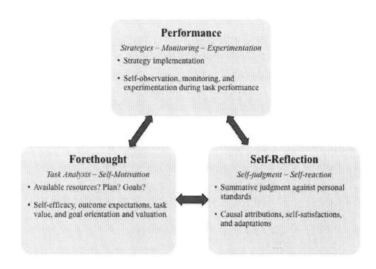

meet those goals. Goal setting is a common thread and enables a feedback loop between the three phases of self-regulation and therefore is an important component of self-regulated learning. Another process involved in the forethought phase, self-motivation, includes a number of motivational states and processes including goal orientation and valuation, self-efficacy, outcome expectations, and task value.

Given the ease of learning for gifted students, gifted underachievers might feel they do not need to plan a project or, when they do plan, may not be able to set appropriate academic goals. Often it is significant others, typically parents or teachers, who establish goals for students or who convince students that they need to plan when approaching a complex task. Teachers and parents, therefore, provide some initial guidance regarding the organization of the project and goal setting. In addition, these significant others help students find relevance in the task and offset negative self-efficacy. Thus, self-regulation in this phase emerges out of social interactions designed to support good decision making on the part of the student. Gifted underachievers, however, may view academic achievement as their parents' or teachers' goal rather than their own.[23]

Research on achieving and underachieving gifted students indicates that students' goal valuation—valuing the goals of school—is an important factor in determining whether a student achieves.[24] Further, McCoach and Siegle[25] found that student motivation and goal valuation were highly correlated, which suggests the existence of a relationship between students' goals and their motivation to complete them, and that goal valuation and motivation were statistically significant predictors of whether a student was considered to be a gifted achiever or gifted underachiever.

There are also goals that are linked to students' beliefs about the stability and controllability of intelligence. For instance, students may be steered by goals to achieve mastery or to show high ability. Students with a mastery goal orientation believe that ability can be increased through effort and will not judge themselves in comparison to peers.[26] In general, they are more likely to self-monitor, use a larger variety of strategies, have higher self-efficacy, have more interest in academic tasks and attribute success to increased effort.[27] Similarly, students who view academic outcomes as controllable are more likely to be persistent, have high self-efficacy, and to be intrinsically motivated.[28] In contrast, a student with a performance goal orientation believes that ability is stable and fixed. This student's goal is to promote either the perception of high ability or avoid the perception of low ability.[29] Such students, who seek to show high ability or, at least, avoid appearing incompetent, select easy tasks or tasks that allow them a competitive edge.[30]

Research on gifted achievers indicates that they tend to adopt a mastery goal orientation, whereas gifted underachieving students tend to adopt a performance goal orientation.[31] Gifted underachievers, who want to be winners and avoid losing, may not put forth sufficient effort due to their fear of failure. They might also set goals either too high or too low in order to guarantee failure. This is a defense mechanism that allows for the student to place blame somewhere outside of him or herself.[32] In addition having high mastery goals serves as a protective factor for those gifted achievers who base their self-esteem on academic outcomes. For these students, mastery goals can serve as moderators between the students' perceived gap between personal standards and performance and their academic self-efficacy.[33]

A student's self-efficacy is important for motivation in the forethought phase.[34] Perceived self-efficacy is a student's judgment of his or her capabilities to organize and implement a course of action needed to learn or perform.[35] Students with high self-efficacy will set more challenging goals, often experience improvements in strategy use, and will put forth more effort.[36] Not surprisingly, the self-efficacy of gifted students depends on the content area, with students having higher levels of self-efficacy in the content area in which they are gifted, but lower self-efficacy in other areas.[37] For example, a student who is gifted in mathematics might feel capable of doing well on tasks in mathematics but may have low expectations for success in literature. When gifted underachievers experience failure, they can begin to feel less and less capable. As their fear of failure increases,

13

their self-efficacy may decrease.[38] When this occurs, these students may feel that they are incapable of achieving in the domain in which they are experiencing failure, even if they put forth more effort.

Task value also influences student motivation and performance and has been defined as the importance of doing well on the task, the enjoyment gained by performing the task, the usefulness of the task, and the cost of the task.[39] When students value a task, they are more likely to put forth more effort and experience higher levels of academic achievement.[40] However, as gifted underachievers get older, they might begin to lose interest in school, find school boring, and begin to value other activities and interests more than their schoolwork.[41]

Performance phase. The performance phase incorporates processes and formative assessments that take place during the execution of the task at hand. These assessments allow students to monitor their performance while they implement strategies and observe their behavior. During this phase, performance monitoring occurs through self-controlled implementation of chosen strategies, ongoing observation of one's and peers' performance, and self-experimentation to test hypotheses made during observations.

Self-control is the purposeful implementation of the strategies that were identified during the forethought phase.[42] Zimmerman[43] identified a few salient methods of self-control including imagery, self-instruction, attention focusing, and task strategies. These strategies can include using study techniques (e.g., acronyms or word associations) or carefully choosing or creating an environment that is more conducive to the particular needs of the student and the task (e.g., quiet, less-stimulation, turning phone off, brightly lit, large work space).

As self-regulated students implement these strategies, they use self-observation and self-experimentation to help them meet their goals. Self-observation, which is already a common habit of gifted students,[44] occurs when students consciously monitor their own performance for patterns and efficiency. An important feature of this self-observation is the act of self-recording in the form of writing down strategies used and the resulting outcomes.[45] For example, a student may note that it takes him or her more time to read a chapter on a computer or hand-held tablet than it does if the material is printed. Self-experimentation helps students test hypotheses developed during their self-observations. For example, the student may choose to conduct a self-experiment to test a hypothesis that reading on the computer is slower by timing how fast he or she is able to read a page of text and how often he or she has to re-read a section on both mediums. The results of such observation, ideally, will help to better inform more effective strategy choices in the future.

Monitoring also can involve social comparisons with others' performance or awareness of others' reactions to one's own performance. Students improve their performance through vicarious learning that involves modeling other people's successful behavior,[46] which also can improve motivation. After observing a model, which could be a teacher or peer, a student is more likely to become motivated if he or she believes a change in behavior will improve performance. In this way, teacher and peer modeling of self-regulated learning strategies can improve both self-efficacy and student performance.[47] Schunk[48] found that comparative information about other students' performance increased motivation, and students who set goals and socially compared outcomes achieved the highest. Such social comparisons not only motivate students but also can provide valuable peer modeling of more efficient or effective strategies.

Self-reflection phase. This phase of self-regulation involves students' summative judgment of their performance against personal standards. According to Zimmerman's[49] model, the self-reflection phase includes components of self-judgment and self-reactions. The components of self-judgment are self-evaluation and causal attributions, and the components of self-reactions are self-satisfactions and adaptations. Ultimately, self-judgments provide necessary evidence to support a student's adaptations of future strategies.

Self-judgment. Self-regulating students, having set certain standards or goals for different components of the learning process, use these goals to compare the products of their learning and make summative decisions about the effectiveness of strategies and whether change needs to occur in future attempts.[50] When students evaluate performance, attributions will be made to explain the outcome, especially if the outcome is unexpected, negative, or particularly important. The students' interpretations are connected to their affective state and are reliant on the students' attribution of their successes and failures to internal or external, stable or unstable, and controllable or uncontrollable factors. As a whole, gifted students attribute general academic success to their hard work and high ability while attributing academic failure to not working hard enough, not completing work in the correct way, and task difficulty.[51] While periodic failure may not be indicative of a poor attributional pattern,[52] chronic underachievers may be held back by a belief that effort is not important and that it is not important for strategy use.[53] When these students experience challenging tasks, they might attribute their difficulty to lack of intelligence. They may view students who work harder at such tasks as less intelligent than students who can perform without putting forth any effort.[54] Further, when gifted underachieving students begin to feel a lack of control over success, they may experience defensive reactions to failure.[55]

Self-reaction. Self-reactions, by way of rewards or punishments for performance, also can have a motivating effect on subsequent work. Sometimes, the reaction is simply a feeling of satisfaction or dissatisfaction. Other times, it can be an external or tangible reward such as a study break, movie, or purchasing something they desire. Positive rewards for authentic achievement are obvious motivators but negative reactions can also be motivating if the individual believes that he or she is capable of doing better. Studies have shown that the use of such self-reactions (positive or negative) is a significant predictor among high-achieving, teenaged students of academic achievement and an intention to pursue post-secondary education.[56] Among gifted underachievers, those who have adopted a performance goal orientation and do not believe that they can overcome failure through effort might try to deflect blame. They might blame others for their failure, avoid competition out of fear of failure, feel helpless and incapable, experience even less interest in school, and discontinue academic effort.[57]

Underachievement, particularly in gifted students, can be frustrating for parents and teachers. The discrepancy between potential and performance level represents a loss of student achievement and development. While underachievement can be caused by a variety of factors, high-ability students often have not developed the self-regulatory skills needed to succeed in a more challenging academic environment. This self-regulated learning model provides a framework for students, parents, and teachers to identify potential gaps in skills that may be affecting student success. Once identified, intervention efforts can be put into place to help these special students reach their potential.

RECOMMENDED INTERVENTIONS

Interventions aimed at improving student implementation of self-regulated learning strategies focus on improving processes within the three phases of self-regulated learning. These interventions focus on goal setting, self-monitoring, peer and teacher modeling, and feedback. The following methods and strategies described by Zimmerman, Bonner, and Kovach[58] and Zimmerman[59] have been effective in helping teachers develop components of the three phases of self-regulated learning in their students.

Forethought Phase:

1. Students set and record goals for upcoming assignments including homework, class assignments, quizzes, and tests. Goals should be short-term, specific, and mastery oriented in order to have the greatest impact on students' self-efficacy, effort, and persistence. Teacher encourages effort by finding tasks that are of interest to these students.

2. Students record self-efficacy related to set goals (i.e., their confidence in being able to meet their goal).

3. Teacher emphasizes the importance of using strategies to meet goals and instructs students on possible strategies to improve learning, models the goal setting process, and encourages students to be very specific about strategy choice.

4. Students record specific strategies they have chosen to use in order to meet their goal. Teacher encourages students to break complex tasks into smaller, more manageable parts.

Performance Phase:

1. Students implement the specific strategies chosen, and monitor how effectively they implement each strategy. Monitoring involves comparison between specific short-term goals and outcomes.
2. Teacher offers daily opportunities for students to practice strategies directed toward a learning goal.
3. Students have opportunities to offer feedback to their peers. Feedback should be detailed with a discussion of how the student is progressing toward his/her learning goals. Assignments and strategies used to complete assignments can be shared, and students can recommend alternative strategies.
4. The teacher offers feedback to students regarding strategies chosen, including a detailed discussion of progress toward meeting learning goal.

Self-Reflection Phase:

1. Students are offered multiple opportunities to compare outcomes to long-term learning goals and reflect on the effectiveness of strategies implemented.
2. Teacher and students discuss causal attributions (i.e., a student's attribution of success or failure) based on student outcomes, with a focus on effort rather than ability. This form of feedback can improve student self-efficacy as students begin to attribute success to effort.
3. Teacher and peers provide feedback in order to make improvements on strategy choice and implementation. Again, feedback should be

detailed and should include a discussion of how the student is progressing toward long-term learning goals.

4. Teacher shares exemplary models of strategy choice and effective implementation.

5. Teacher and students discuss choice of strategies as students move back to forethought phase and set new goals, record self-efficacy related to goals, and record strategies to be implemented.

Possible Student Strategies to Improve Performance:

- Organize and transform information – make an outline, use a concept map, create flashcards, highlight important information.
- Seek information – go to the library or Internet.
- Seek help – ask for help from peers, teachers, or other adults.
- Review records – read over notes or complete practice problems when preparing for a test.
- Rehearse and memorize – use flashcards, use mnemonic devices, create sample problems or questions, tutor a peer.
- Structure environment appropriately – reduce distractions, set regular study time and place, prioritize tasks. This strategy allows for attention focusing.
- Keep records – take notes, make lists, keep a notebook or journal. Keeping records is an important aspect of self-monitoring and is necessary as students evaluate effectiveness of strategies chosen.

- Self-reward – earn a personal reward for high performance. This strategy should improve students' self-satisfaction.
- Self-evaluate – check over work, analyze errors. An aspect of self-judgment, positive self-evaluation based on effort, improves causal attributions and gives students a sense of self-satisfaction.

While teachers initiate the intervention by instructing students to use self-regulated learning strategies, the intention is for students, over time, to begin to use these strategies on their own without direct instruction from the teacher. Students should begin to record goals, strategies, and progress toward implementing their strategies and meeting their goals. Practicing the task strategies listed above should improve students' self-control and help with self-observation, which should, in turn, contribute to positive self-evaluations. Students should begin to attribute their increased performance to effort rather than ability and experience positive self-reactions, which should improve self-efficacy. As students enter into the next forethought phase, they should set higher goals, experience more interest in the given academic domain, and put forth more effort. Zimmerman[60] recommends shifting the responsibility of learning to the students, while the teacher develops the self-regulated learner by modeling procedures for self-monitoring and selection of strategies. Because helping students develop self-regulated learning skills can be difficult due to the time it takes for students to practice the strategies and develop new habits, teachers need to be patient and implement the strategies over time. The strategies for students and interventions to be used by teachers are illustrated with two typical cases of high school gifted underachievers as examples.

Case 1: Harper

Due to Harper's history of not completing homework assignments, Mr. Perry encourages Harper to make this a focus as she sets goals and chooses strategies to prepare for the next test. Although Harper has been failing recent tests, she is determined to make an A on the next one. Harper decides to set a goal of spending 30 minutes per day on her homework assignments in calculus. When Mr. Perry gives students an opportunity to compare their progress toward meeting their goals, Harper realizes that most of her peers spend much more time on calculus each day. Harper, however, does not enjoy doing homework, so she remains hopeful that her efforts will be enough. Due to Mr. Perry's request, she keeps a record of the time spent on homework every day, and she notices that while some days she is easily able to work for 30 minutes, on other days she is easily distracted, too busy with other activities, or she simply forgets. Over a 12-day period she is able to work on her homework for 30 minutes on 7 of the 12 days. She does not make an A on the test as she had hoped, but she does see some improvement, earning a grade of 78. During self-reflection time set aside by Mr. Perry after the test, Harper begins to see that increased effort on homework may be having a positive influence on her understanding and performance. Mr. Perry gives feedback to Harper that includes recommendations for improving her strategy choices by being more specific about how she will ensure that she will spend the necessary time each night preparing for calculus. She decides to work during a set time every evening at the kitchen table, and she has increased her study time to

*one hour based on feedback from her peers. She
communicates to her parents and family that this is a time
when she needs to be free from distraction and elicits their
help in staying on task. She also has asked one of her friends
if she would like to work on calculus together when either of
them needs help, and she and her friend have agreed to be
available to each other by phone when necessary. While she
is still a little unsure of her success, she is a little more
confident now that she has set more specific goals for herself
for the coming weeks.*

Harper and Mr. Perry have effectively implemented
several of the strategies recommended to improve self-
regulation. Harper has begun to keep records, structure her
environment appropriately, and seek help. Mr. Perry has
encouraged specific goal setting with Harper's goal of
studying for calculus 30 minutes every day. He also
prompted her to self-monitor by recording the time spent on
homework daily and allowed time for peer modeling and
feedback as students compared progress toward meeting
goals. Harper is allowed class time for self-reflection, during
which she is given feedback and after which she moves back
into goal setting with an improved level of self-efficacy based
on her attribution of success to effort.

In addition to the recommended strategies for teachers
and students, several other aspects of self-regulated learning
may be able to help students like Harper. For example,
students need to learn to manage their time effectively
throughout the self-regulation cycle. In addition, effective
note taking, which includes both recording and revision, can
greatly impact students' understanding and performance.
When students take notes they must focus on the most
important information and during revision use strategies to

reorganize their notes in outlines, tables, or concept maps. Homework completion, proper time management, and effective note taking are the foundations of preparing for a test. To prepare for an exam, students and teachers should apply the strategies listed above in order to help students complete assignments, prepare for quizzes, review for the exam, and learn from students' performance on the exam. These additional aspects of self-regulation can be implemented with the guidance of the three phases of the self-regulated learning cycle described above, during which the teacher can encourage students to self-monitor these strategies over a period of time. Based on the expectancy-value theory of motivation, it is also recommended that the ability level of the student should match the difficulty level of the task, and the teacher should offer task choices whenever possible to encourage student interest.[61] Again, Harper is used as an example of how teachers can effectively implement these strategies in their classrooms.

After fine-tuning her efforts toward completing homework assignments for calculus, Harper has begun to understand the importance of putting forth effort for improving performance. After students have practiced and refined the self-regulation cycle for several weeks with their initial goals, Mr. Perry decides his students need to focus on improvement of note-taking skills and test preparation. While Harper does take notes in calculus, she often feels it is unnecessary and just listens when Mr. Perry is teaching a concept. However, with Mr. Perry's encouragement, she sets a new goal of always taking notes during these lectures. With her improved self-efficacy, driven by her increased performance after spending more time completing homework assignments, Harper feels confident that she will be able to meet her goal of improved note taking. Mr. Perry has decided to prepare guided notes for each concept, which provides a framework in which students may add their own notes. Also, periodically, Mr. Perry sets aside class time for students to revise their notes by making an outline, using a concept map, creating flashcards, or highlighting important information, and he offers exemplars of each to the students. Mr. Perry has also requested that students set mastery goals rather than performance goals. As he would like for students to focus on mastery of the content in calculus rather than making a certain grade, he gives the students feedback related to the content. Feedback is given on each quiz and includes information about content areas in which the students are doing well, and specific information about areas where students are struggling.

Harper keeps track of her note taking using a chart provided by Mr. Perry, and she is given several opportunities to compare the quality of her notes and revision techniques with her peers. In addition to revision techniques, Mr. Perry also presents several test preparation strategies including peer tutoring and quizzing, mnemonic devices, and error analysis. Harper decides to continue to work with her homework study partner as she prepares for her test. The two students decide to meet every evening for several days to compare notes, quiz each other, and practice problems in order to prepare for the test.

Before and during the test, Harper experiences some test anxiety, but she notices that it is lower than before. She feels much more confident that she will perform at a higher level based on her improved time management, note-taking, and test preparation skills. She receives an 85 on her test, but more importantly she knows she has a much better understanding of the content. Implementation of the above *strategies was not perfect. Harper experienced several setbacks along the way, but based on feedback from her peers and Mr. Perry, she is working on making improvements in strategy choice and implementation. Harper has found that giving rewards to herself, such as shopping with her friends, is a good motivator for her after a week of meeting her goals. Harper is feeling less pressured and frustrated and she has a newfound motivation to put forth effort and persevere when challenged. Not only is Harper doing better in class, but she is also more interested in calculus and understands the value of the tasks assigned by Mr. Perry. She is beginning to attribute her success to her increased efforts rather than innate ability and she no longer feels like giving up.*

Both Mr. Perry and Harper show progress toward effective implementation of self-regulated learning strategies. Harper is becoming competent at setting proximal, specific, mastery goals and monitoring progress toward meeting those goals. Through observation of Mr. Perry, her peers, and through self-observation she is increasing her list of appropriately executed strategies. She understands the importance of effort, and has an increased self-efficacy for performance in calculus. Throughout the cycle she monitors her progress toward meeting her goals, and makes changes to strategies when needed, rewarding herself with a shopping trip with friends. The class culture has shifted from a competitive, performance focus to one based on effort and aimed at meeting goals of mastering course content.

Case 2: Steven

Due to Steven's real surprise and lack of concern at doing poorly and his many excuses to defend his behavior, Mrs. Torres encourages Steven to set sub-goals and monitor acquisition of these goals. It seems that in the past Steven's goal was simply to get by and avoid responsibility, so Mrs. Torres decides to make it nearly impossible for Steven to make any more excuses by encouraging him to monitor his effort. Mrs. Torres has assigned a project requiring students to read a book and write a reflection paper about the assigned reading. In the past Mrs. Torres has required all students to read the same book, but for this year's assignment she has decided to allow students to choose from a list of approved books in order to increase student interest. With encouragement, Steven decides to set two sub-goals: reading for 30 minutes per day, and writing in his reflection journal for 15 minutes per day. Unfortunately, Steven finds it difficult to meet his goals. When Mrs. Torres gives the class an opportunity to compare their progress toward meeting their goals, Steven realizes that he has been spending time with his friends rather than doing his assigned reading and reflection. Based on the records, which Mrs. Torres is requiring her students to keep on progress toward meeting their goals, he realizes that he read for a total of two hours over an entire week and completed his reflection only once. When it is time for the books to be completed and to begin the reflection paper, Steven has finished only half of the assigned reading. While Steven has not met his goal, Mrs. Torres chooses to see this as an improvement since previously Steven had not completed any of the assigned readings. During self-reflection time set aside by Mrs. Torres, Steven begins to see that it is his own choices that are keeping him from completing his assignments. Mrs. Torres gives feedback to Steven, including praise for improving his commitment to completing the assigned reading and encouragement for trying to spend the pre-set time on his reading and reflection every evening. She also develops a plan with Steven and his parents in which Steven will stay

*after school every day for an additional hour until he has
caught up on his reading.*

Steven and Mrs. Torres have effectively implemented a
few of the strategies recommended to improve self-
regulation. Steven has begun to keep records and Mrs.
Torres has encouraged specific goal setting, offered
feedback, and provided opportunities for her students to
compare outcomes to their goals. However, the
responsibility for learning has not yet shifted from the
teacher to the student. Mrs. Torres can help Steven develop
as a self-regulated learner by modeling procedures and
continuing to remain patient as it takes time for Steven to
create new habits.

*Steven has just begun to understand the importance of
putting forth effort. He is able to catch up on his assigned
reading by staying after school daily with Mrs. Torres and
has now completed most of his reflections. Mrs. Torres
models the process of outlining the reflection papers and she
sets aside class time for students to provide peer feedback on
several drafts of their papers. Mrs. Torres also continues to
allow time for students to discuss their progress toward
meeting their daily goals. After completing his reading
assignments and receiving feedback from his peers and Mrs.
Torres, Steven set a goal to spend 45 minutes daily working
on his reflection paper, and he decides to stay after school
several days a week in order to increase his productivity.
Before students complete their last draft, Mrs. Torres shares
several exemplary papers from past years with her students
and explains how she graded these papers using the grading
rubric. Steven performs very well on his reflection paper, but
most importantly he has really begun to understand the
importance of effort and his responsibility in completing his*

assignments. Although Steven did not completely meet his daily goals, he has stopped making excuses for the time he spent doing something besides preparing for his literature class.

Both Mrs. Torres and Steven have begun to successfully implement several self-regulated learning strategies. Steven is becoming successful at setting sub-goals, monitoring progress toward meeting those goals, and making adaptations to his plan as needed. He has been able to put off spending time with his friends until he has completed his daily assignments for literature class. Mrs. Torres has modeled the correct use of self-regulation strategies and has allowed time for her students to practice these strategies.

CONCLUSION

Self-regulation appears to play an important role in the academic achievement of the gifted student. Gifted underachievers may not implement self-regulation strategies for many reasons, including low self-efficacy, lack of strategy knowledge, and unrealistic expectations. Self-regulatory processes are teachable and teachers can help gifted underachievers see that they can improve their performance with increased effort. When gifted children are trained in strategy use, they use strategies better than their non-gifted peers and also are able to transfer the strategies to novel situations.[62] In addition to the strategies listed above, Zimmerman, Bonner, and Kovach[63] recommend that teachers should be prepared to answer questions from students as they experience changes in the classroom. Teachers need to be clear about their expectation of students related to self-regulated learning, and they need to plan these interventions as they would plan curricular components. It is important to consider that no learning intervention is effective with all students all of the time; teachers need to continue to evaluate their effectiveness and set new goals, and they need to ensure that the difficulty level of the task matches the ability level of the student. In heterogeneous classrooms this task may be more difficult, and training in differentiation of instruction may be necessary. Students may not learn these skills overnight, but over time the gifted underachiever may begin to practice these skills alone with little direction from the teacher. As students become self-regulated learners, they should begin to use the newly learned strategies appropriately in novel learning situations and experience improvements in the use of self-regulated learning strategies, self-efficacy, and content knowledge.

ENDNOTES

[1] Zimmerman, B. J. (2002). Becoming a self-regulated learner: An overview. *Theory into Practice, 41*, 64-70.

[2] Zimmerman, 2002.

[3] Zimmerman, B. J. (1990). Self-regulated learning and academic achievement: An overview. *Educational Psychologist, 25*, 3-17.

[4] Rubenstein, L. D., Siegle, D., Reis, S. M., McCoach, D. B., & Burton, M. G. (2012). A complex quest: The development and research of underachievement interventions for gifted students. *Psychology in the Schools, 49*, 678-694.

[5] Schunk, D.H., & Zimmerman, B.J. (Eds.). (1998). *Self-regulated learning: From teaching to self-reflective practice*. New York, NY: Guilford Press.

[6] Reis, S. M., & McCoach, D. B. (2000). The underachievement of gifted students: What do we know and where do we go? *Gifted Child Quarterly, 44*, 152-170.

[7] Yssel, N., Adams, C., Clarke, L. S., & Jones, R. (2014). Applying an RTI model for students with learning disabilities. *Teaching Exceptional Children, 46*(3), 42-52.

[8] Renzulli, J., & Park, S. (2000). Gifted dropouts: The who and the why. *Gifted Child Quarterly, 44*, 261-271.

[9] Richert, E. S. (1991). Rampant problems and promising practices in identification. In N. Colangelo & G. A. Davis (Eds.), *Handbook of gifted education* (pp. 81–96). Boston, MA: Allyn & Bacon.

[10] Rimm, S. (2008). *Why bright kids get poor grades—and what you can do about it*. Scottsdale, AZ: Great Potential Press.

[11] Reis & McCoach, 2000.

[12] Reis & McCoach, 2000.

[13] Dweck, C. S. (2006). *Mindset: The new psychology of success*. New York, NY: Random House; Snyder, K. E., & Linnenbrink-Garcia, L. (2013). A developmental person-centered approach to exploring multiple motivational pathways to gifted underachievement. *Educational Psychologist, 48*, 209-228.

[14] Snyder, K. E., Malin, J. L., Dent, A. L., & Linnenbrink-Garcia, L. (2014). The message matters: The role of implicit beliefs about giftedness and failure experiences in academic self-handicapping. *Journal of Educational Psychology, 106*, 230-241.

[15] Rimm, 2008.

[16] Dweck, 2006.

[17] Hettinger & Knapp (2001). Potential, performance, and paradox: A case study of J.P., a verbally gifted struggling reader. *Journal for the Education of the Gifted, 24*, 248-289.

[18] Zimmerman, 2002.

[19] Zimmerman, B. J. (2001). Theories of self-regulated learning and academic achievement. In B. J. Zimmerman & D. H. Schunk (Eds.), *Self-regulated learning and academic achievement* (pp. 1-38). Mahway, NJ: Erlbaum.

[20] Boekaerts, M., & Corno, L. (2005). Self-regulation in the classroom: A perspective on assessment and intervention. *Applied Psychology: An International Review, 54*, 199-231.

[21] Zimmerman, 2002.

[22] Zimmerman, 2002.

[23] Rimm, 2008.

[24] McCoach, D. B., & Siegle, D. (2003). Factors that differentiate underachieving gifted students from high-achieving gifted students. *Gifted Child Quarterly, 47*, 144-154; Rubenstein et al., 2012

[25] McCoach & Siegle, 2003.

[26] Wang, K. T., Fu, C., & Rice, K. G. (2012). Perfectionism in gifted students: Moderating effects of goal orientation and contingent self-worth. *School Psychology Quarterly, 27*, 96-108.

[27] Pintrich, P. R. (2005). The role of goal orientation in self-regulated learning. In M. Boekaerts, P. Pintrich, & M. Zeidner (Eds). *Handbook of self-regulation* (pp. 13-39). San Diego, CA: Academic Press.

[28] Hulleman, C. S., Schrager, S. M., Bodmann, S. M., & Harackiewicz, J. M. (2010). A meta analytic review of achievement goal measures: Different labels for the same constructs or different constructs with similar labels? *Psychological Bulletin, 136*, 422-449.

[29] Pintrich, 2005; Wang, et al., 2012.

[30] Speirs Neumeister, K. L. (2004). Understanding the relationship between perfectionism and achievement motivation in gifted college students. *Gifted Child Quarterly, 48*, 219-231.

[31] Albaili, M. A. (2003). Motivational goal orientations of intellectually gifted achieving and underachieving students in

the United Arab Emirates. *Social Behavior and Personality, 31*(2), 107-120.

[32] Rimm, 2008.

[33] Wang et al., 2012.

[34] Zimmerman, 2001.

[35] Bandura, A. B. (1997). *Self-efficacy: The exercise of control.* New York, NY: Freeman.

[36] Bandura, 1997.

[37] Clinkenbeard, P. R. (2012). Motivation of gifted students: Implications of theory and research. *Psychology in the Schools, 49*, 622-630.

[38] Rimm, 2008.

[39] Wigfield, A., & Eccles, J. S. (2000). Expectancy-value theory of achievement motivation. *Contemporary Educational Psychology, 25*, 68-81.

[40] Wigfield & Eccles, 2000.

[41] Rimm, 2008.

[42] Zimmerman, 2002.

[43] Zimmerman, 2002.

[44] Burney, V. H. (2008). Applications of social cognitive theory to gifted education. *Roeper Review, 30*, 130-139.

[45] Cleary, T. J., & Zimmerman, B. J. (2004). Self-regulation empowerment program: A school- based program to enhance self-regulated and self-motivated cycles of student learning. *Psychology in the Schools, 41*, 537-550.

[46] Schunk, D. (2008). *Learning theories: An educational perspective* (5th ed.). Upper Saddle River, NJ: Pearson.

[47] Zimmerman, B. J. (1989). A social cognitive view of self-regulated academic learning. *Journal of Educational Psychology, 81*, 329-339.

[48] Schunk, 1983b, as cited in Schunk, 2008.

[49] Zimmerman, 2002.

[50] Mega, C., Ronconi, L., & De Beni, R. (2013). What makes a good student? How emotions, self-regulated learning, and motivation contribute to academic achievement. *Journal of Educational Psychology, 106*, 1-11.

[51] Assouline, S. G., Colangelo, N., Ihrig, D., & Forstadt, L. (2006). Attributional choices for academic success and failure by intellectually gifted students. *Gifted Child Quarterly, 50*, 283-294; see also Dai, D. Y., Moon, S. M., & Feldhusen, J. F.

(1998). Achievement motivation and gifted students: A social cognitive perspective. *Educational Psychologist, 33*, 45-63.

[51] Assouline et al., 2006.

[53] Carr, M., Borkowski, J. G., & Maxwell, S. E. (1991). Motivational components of underachievement. *Developmental Psychology, 27*, 108-118.

[54] Siegle, D., & McCoach, D. B. (2005). *Motivating gifted students*. Waco, TX: Prufrock Press.

[55] Rimm, 2008.

[56] Nota, L., Soresi, S., & Zimmerman, B.J. (2004). Self-regulation and academic achievement and resilience: A longitudinal study. *International Journal of Educational Research, 41*, 198-215.

[57] Rimm, 2008.

[58] Zimmerman, B. J., Bonner, S., & Kovach, R. (1996). *Developing self-regulated learners: Beyond achievement to self-efficacy*. Washington, DC: American Psychological Association.

[59] Zimmerman, 1989.

[60] Zimmerman, et al., 1996.

[61] Clinkenbeard, 2012.

[62] Scruggs & Mastropieri, 1986 & 1988, as cited in Risemberg, R., & Zimmerman, B. J. (1992). Self-regulated learning in gifted students. *Roeper Review, 15*, 98-101.

[63] Zimmerman et al., 1996.

RESOURCES

1. The National Research Center on the Gifted and Talented (NRC/GT) at the University of Connecticut developed a training module on self-regulation and self-regulation intervention. It includes a concise overview of the components of Zimmerman's model of self-regulation, strategies to increase self-regulation, and classroom lessons designed to assist teachers in instructing students on how to develop their own self-regulatory skills.

Greene, M. & Reis, S. M. (n.d.). *Self-Regulation.* Downloaded from http://www.gifted.uconn.edu/Siegle/SelfRegulation/INDEX.HTM

2. Reis, S. M., & Greene, M. J. (n.d.). *Using self-regulated learning to reverse underachievement in talented students*. Downloaded from http://www.gifted.uconn.edu/general/faculty/reis/Self-Regulated_Learning_Reverse_Underachievement.html

3. Dr. Howard Everson, professor of educational psychology and director of the Center for Advanced Study in Education at City University of New York, provides a brief and informative overview of Barry Zimmerman's research and work with self-regulated learning theory and underachieving students. This article is published as a part of a continually updated website called Learning and the Adolescent Mind, a cooperative effort between the University of Texas at Austin and Agile Mind, Inc., to disseminate knowledge about student success to teachers and parents.

Everson, H. (n.d.). *Barry Zimmerman*. Downloaded from http://learningandtheadolescentmind.org/people_04.html

4. For additional information about underachieving gifted students, Hoagies' Gifted Education Page provides a diverse collection of anecdotal and research-based resources for exploring this complex issue. See http://www.hoagiesgifted.org/underachievement.htm

ABOUT THE AUTHORS

Alicia M. Welch is a Ph.D. student in educational psychology at the University of Georgia. She has a bachelor's degree in music performance and a master's degree in higher education and is interested in the development of and interventions for attention skills in preschool students.

Jennifer L. Roth is a Ph.D. student in educational psychology at the University of Georgia. She has a master's degree in mathematics education and was a high school mathematics teacher for 11. Her research interests include student motivation and self-regulation.

Hillary H. Steiner, Ph.D., is assistant professor of educational psychology and assistant director of learning communities at Kennesaw State University, where she works exclusively with first-year college students. Her interests include metacognition, self-regulation, and integrative learning in the college curriculum.

Martha M. Carr, Ph.D., is the Aderhold Distinguished Professor of Educational Psychology, and research fellow, at the University of Georgia Institute of Behavioral Research. She studies the factors that promote mathematics in elementary school. Her first work focused on the application of self-regulating theory to mathematics. Her current research examines how factors combine to influence the development of more advanced mathematical skills.

ABOUT THE SERIES EDITOR

Cheryll M. Adams, Ph.D., is the director emerita of the Center for Gifted Studies and Talent Development at Ball State University. She has served on the Board of Directors of NAGC and has been president of the Indiana Association for the Gifted and the Association for the Gifted, Council for Exceptional Children.

Made in the USA
San Bernardino, CA
28 April 2016